LIVES
AND
TIMES

Mother Teresa

John Barraclough

Heinemann Interactive Library,
Des Plaines, Illinois

© 1998 Reed Educational & Professional Publishing Ltd

Published by Heinemann Interactive Library,
an imprint of Reed Educational & Professional Publishing,
1350 East Touhy Avenue, Suite 240 West
Des Plaines, IL 60018

Produced by Times Offset (M) Sdn. Bhd.
Designed by Ken Vail Graphic Design.
Illustrations by Barbara Lofthouse

02 01 00 99 98
10 9 8 7 6 5 4 3 2 1

Library of Congress Cataloguing-in-Publication Data

Barraclough, John, 1960-
    Mother Teresa / John Barraclough.
        p. cm. --(Lives and times)
    Includes bibliographical references and index.
    ISBN 1-57572-562-2
    1. Teresa, Mother, 1910- --Juvenile literature. 2. Nuns--India--Calcutta--
Biography--Juvenile literature. 3. Missionaries of Charity--Biography--Juvenile
literature. I. Title. II. Series: Lives and times (Crystal Lake, I11.)
BX4406.5.Z8B37 1997
271'.97--dc21   97-16133
                                                                        CIP
                                                                        AC

Some words are shown in bold, **like this**.
You can find out what they mean by looking
in the glossary. The glossary also helps you say
difficult words.

Acknowledgments
The author and publishers are grateful to the following for permission to reproduce copyright photographs:
Andes Press Agency/Carlos Reyes – Manzo, p. 19; Camera Press Ltd / S.K. Dutt, pp. 17, 18, 22

Cover photograph: Popperfoto

Special thanks to Betty Root for her comments in the preparation of this book.

Contents

Part One

Mother Teresa was born in 1910 in Albania. At that time she was called Agnes **Bejaxhiu**. When she was a little girl, Agnes talked to many **missionaries**. She wanted to help people.

When she was 18, Agnes became a **nun**. She was called Sister Teresa. She went to India to be a teacher. She loved her work. But it upset her that so many people lived in **slums**.

Sister Teresa felt that God wanted her to help people. She left the girls' school where she was working. Sister Teresa started a very simple **clinic** where she could help sick people in the **slums**.

The children who lived in the slums had no schools to go to. Sister Teresa started to teach them in the street. She scratched with a stick in the dust the letters of the alphabet.

Two years later, Sister Teresa asked
some other **nuns** to work with her. Her
name became Mother Teresa. All the
nuns wore blue and white robes, like
long, simple dresses.

One day, Mother Teresa found a dying
woman in the street. She had to beg a
hospital to let the homeless woman in.
The woman would have died out in the
street, otherwise.

Mother Teresa knew that she had to do something for the poor people who had no one to help them when they were sick. Nobody should have to die in the street.

In 1952, Mother Teresa opened a home for the **destitute** and dying. This home was called **Kalighat**. Anyone was welcome here, and everyone was cared for.

Mother Teresa has always cared deeply for everyone. She has looked after many children whose parents could not look after them.

In 1955, Mother Teresa and her **nuns** opened a children's home called **Shishu Bavan**. All children can go there and be safe. No matter how full it is, the nuns say, "There is always room for one more."

Lepers are people who have a disease called leprosy. Many lepers are thrown out of their homes. In 1966, Mother Teresa opened a home for lepers in India.

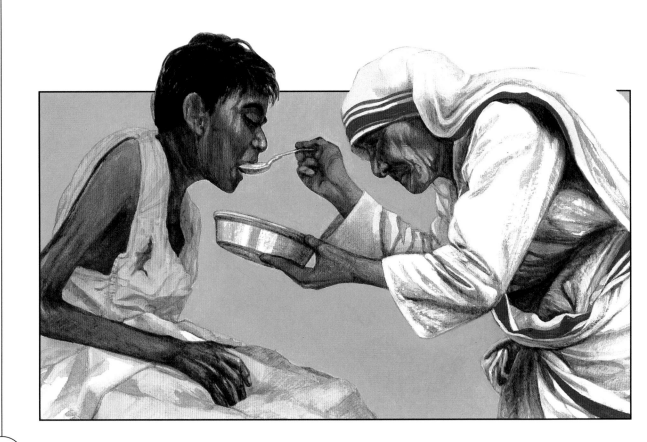

Mother Teresa is famous for her work
with homeless children and people who
are sick and very poor. In 1979, she got an
important prize, called the **Nobel Peace
Prize**. This was to thank her for her work.

Part Two

When Mother Teresa left home to become a **nun** in India, she gave this photograph of herself to her aunt.
It shows what she looked like when she was sixteen.

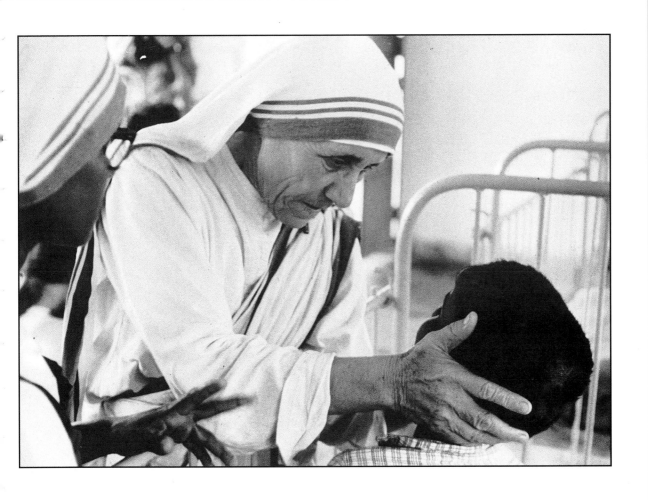

Mother Teresa has worked with the sick and the poor in many places. Her name is known everywhere. There are many photographs of her helping people.

Many photographers have visited the homes opened by Mother Teresa. This is a picture of her **nuns** giving out food.

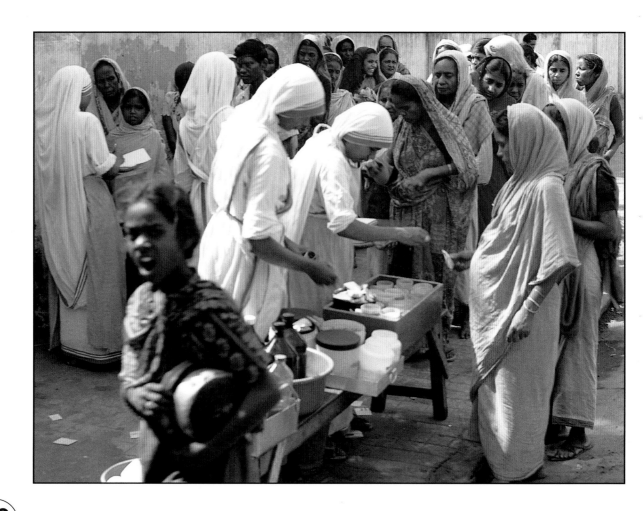

Mother Teresa has worked mainly in India. She has also worked in about 100 other countries. This photograph shows her visiting children in England.

Mother Teresa's friend, Father Henry, kept a scrapbook. It tells us about Mother Teresa. On August 16, 1948, he wrote that Mother Teresa wanted to work with poor people in **Calcutta**.

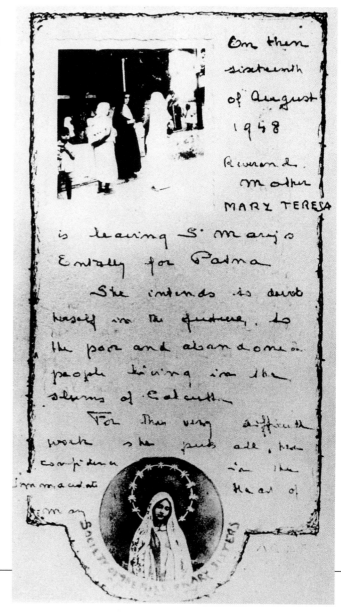

MISSIONARIES OF CHARITY.
54-A, Lower Circular Road,
Calcutta · _____ . 195 .

My dear Mark
Thank you
for your gift.
Love Jesus and
Mary God bless
You & Your Sister
and little Baby
m·Teresa.

Mother Teresa has written many
thank-you letters to people who have
helped with her work. This note is to a
charity that helps people with leprosy.

Kalighat, the home for people who are very poor, and sick or dying, is also called Nirmal Hriday. This means the "Place of the Pure Heart." The sign you can see here is by the entrance to the home.

When Mother Teresa got the **Nobel Peace Prize**, the post office in India made this special stamp. It was a way of thanking her.

Glossary

This glossary explains words, and helps you to say difficult words.

Bejaxhiu You say *BAY sha shoo*.

Calcutta This is a big city in India. You say *kal KUH tuh*.

clinic Place where you go to see a nurse or doctor.

destitute Very poor people are called destitute.

Kalighat You say *KAY lee gat*.

leper Person who has the disease leprosy. You say *LEH pur*.

missionary A missionary is someone who travels to other countries to tell people about his or her religion. You say *MIH shuhn air ee*.

Nobel Peace Prize Prize given to people who have done something very special to help other people.

nun Woman who follows the Christian religion, and who lives as part of a group of nuns. They all follow the same rules. They pray, and often help other people.

Shishu Bavan You say *SHI shoo Bah vahn*.

slums Areas with very poor housing with no running water, electricity, or gas. They are sometimes built from whatever people can find, such as wood, plastic, and corrugated metal.

Index

More Books to Read

Gray, Charlotte. *Mother Teresa: Servant of the World's Suffering People.* Milwaukee: Gareth Stevens, 1990.

Wheeler, Jill. *Mother Teresa.* Edina, Minn.: Alodo, 1992.